INDEPENDENT RESEARCH LIBRARY ACTIVITIES

USING THE DEWEY DECIMAL SYSTEM

By
Harriet Kinghorn
and
Fay Hill Smith

Cover Illustration By
Kathy Rogers

Inside Illustrations By
Darcy Myers

Publishers
T.S. Denison & Company, Inc.
Minneapolis, Minnesota 55431

ACKNOWLEDGMENTS

We want to thank Nancy L. Reed, Bianca I. Katz, and Helen Colella for their help in the preparation of the manuscript.

Standard Book Number: 513-02173-6
Independent Research Library Activities
Copyright © 1992 by T.S. Denison & Co., Inc.
9601 Newton Avenue South
Minneapolis, Minnesota 55431

TEACHER/PARENT NOTES

The collections in many school and public libraries are arranged according to the Dewey Decimal System of classification which was formulated by Melvil Dewey in 1876. A chart of the Dewey Decimal System appears below:

Main Dewey Decimal Classification Groups

000-099	Generalities (encyclopedias, bibliographies, periodicals, journalism)
100-199	Philosophy and Related Disciplines (philosophy, psychology, logic)
200-299	Religion
300-299	The Social Sciences (economics, sociology, civics, law, education, vocations, customs)
400-499	Language (language, dictionaries, grammar)
500-599	Pure Sciences (mathematics, astronomy, physics, chemistry, geology, paleontology, biology, zoology, botany)
600-699	Technology (medicine, engineering, agriculture, home economics, business, radio, television, aviation)
700-799	The Arts (architecture, sculpture, painting, music, photography, recreation)
800-899	Literature (novels, poetry, plays, criticism)
900-999	General Geography and History

Even young learners can become familiar with the Dewey Decimal System and acquire basic research skills. This book provides the appropriate materials, teaching aids, and resource lists to guide children on an informative journey through the library. The sections of *Independent Library Activities* are arranged according to the classifications of the Dewey Decimal System. Each section contains two pages of activities relating to the given classification group. Please note that the categories found within a Dewey Decimal Classification Group (Example: Painting and Music under 700-799: "The Arts") were chosen <u>arbitrarily</u> as appropriate for the elementary student—many other categories are available in addition to those detailed in this resource.

Allow children their own choice of activities (depending on their ages and abilities). The activities involve research, speaking, and writing, and may be used to supplement a unit of study. Encourage the children to use more than one resource for a given activity, and instruct them to copy down the title, author, and call number for each resource that has helped them complete an activity. Children should complete at least half of the given activities and then create their own independent activities, using the reproducible form provided in the back of the book.

The Dewey Decimal charts in the back of the book will also enhance the students' knowledge of the Dewey Decimal System. The charts have pictures to help younger children identify the meaning of the words such as *philosophy*. These charts can be placed on the classroom walls or at learning centers. Once students are familiar with the kinds of books under each classification, you might play a game asking questions such as:

Where would you find information about your favorite birds? (500)

Where would you find books about jazz music? (700)

Where would you find a book about the Hawaiian Islands? (900)

To organize completed work, each student may keep a pocket portfolio. Students may also keep journals in which they record and analyze their experiences. As students complete a project they may summarize their work, note the problems they encountered, and detail ideas which their studies generated.

The following activities require little preparation but provide a wide range of opportunity for experience and learning. The skills acquired through completion of these activities are practical and will be used throughout the students' school years and on into adulthood—for education and for pleasure.

TABLE OF CONTENTS

000–099
GENERALITIES:
REFERENCE BOOKS

Activity 1—Magazine Fun
You will need: Pencil, paper, a current magazine.

Choose a current magazine and read a non-fiction article. Write a paragraph telling what you learned from the article. Be sure to list the name of the magazine you chose, its date of publication, and the page number your article is found on.

Activity 2—Famous People
You will need: Pencil, crayons/markers, paper, biographic reference books.

Choose a famous person who interests you. Using a biographic reference book, learn about that person's life and work. Write a report. Make a time line showing important dates in the person's life.

Activity 3—Museum Reference Books
You will need: Pencil, paper, encyclopedia or other reference books.

In the general section of the library you will find information about the world's museums. Using an encyclopedia or a reference book about museums, list the names and locations of six museums in North America. If the museums have unique or unusual features, list them after the name of the museum.

Activity 4—Web A Topic of Your Choice
You will need: Pencil, paper, reference books.

Read about a topic of your choice. Then draw a web to show information about this topic.

Activity 5—Using an Encyclopedia
You will need: Pencil, crayons/markers, paper, encyclopedia.

Choose an animal that interests you. Use an encyclopedia to learn about the animal. Write a report. Draw and label illustrations to share your information with the class.

Activity 6—Almanacs & Atlases
You will need: Pencil, paper, almanac, atlas.

Look up a list of national monuments in an almanac. List the names and locations of at least five monuments and use an atlas to find their geographic location.

Activity 7—Careers
You will need: Pencil, paper, encyclopedia or other reference books.

Read about a career of your choice. Pretend you are working in this career. Write about what you do each day (or night) that you are at work.

Activity 8—Unnumbered Reference Books
You will need: Pencil, paper, reference books.

In many libraries you can find reference materials that are not numbered. You may find atlases, almanacs, dictionaries, and encyclopedias in this section. These books remain in the library at all times. Look in your school library and list what reference resources are available. Are there any unnumbered reference books in your school library? If so, list them.

GENERALITIES:
REFERENCE BOOKS

Althea. VISITING A MUSEUM. New York: Cambridge University Press, 1983.

Aylesworth, Thomas G. KIDS' ALMANAC OF THE UNITED STATES. New York: Pharos Bks., 1990.

Boughton, Simon. GREAT LIVES. New York: Doubleday, 1988.

Calder, S. J. FIRST FACTS. Illus. by Cornelius Van Wright. Englewood Cliffs, New Jersey: Messner, 1990.

CHILDCRAFT: THE HOW AND WHY LIBRARY. Chicago: World Book, Inc., 1992.

COBBLESTONE, The History Magazine for Young People. Peterborough, New Hampshire: Cobblestone Publishing.

Dempsey, Michael W. STUDENT ATLAS. Mahwah, New Jersey: Troll Assoc., 1991.

Elwood, Ann and Carol O. Madigan. THE MACMILLAN BOOK OF FASCINATING FACTS: AN ALMANAC FOR KIDS. New York: Macmillan Child Group, 1989.

Grisewood, John. THE DOUBLEDAY CHILDREN'S ALMANAC. New York: Doubleday, 1986.

HAMMOND DISCOVERING MAPS: A YOUNG PERSON'S WORLD ATLAS. Maplewood, New Jersey: Hammond Incorporated, 1991.

HAMMOND DISCOVERY WORLD ATLAS. Maplewood, New Jersey: Hammond Incorporated, 1988.

THE KIDS' QUESTION AND ANSWER BOOK. New York: Grosset, 1988.

NATIONAL GEOGRAPHIC WORLD. Washington DC: National Geographic Society.

Papajani, Janet. MUSEUMS. Chicago: Childrens Press, 1989.

Paton, John, ed. PICTURE ENCYCLOPEDIA FOR CHILDREN. New York: Putnam Pub. Group, 1987.

RAND MCNALLY PICTURE ATLAS OF THE WORLD. Illus. by Brian Delf. Chicago: Rand McNally, 1991.

RANGER RICK. Vienna, Virginia: National Wildlife Foundation.

Reynolds, Jean, ed. NEW BOOK OF KNOWLEDGE. Danbury, Connecticut: Grolier Inc., 1989.

Standard Educational Corporation Staff. NEW STANDARD ENCYCLOPEDIA. Chicago: Standard Ed., 1992.

Weil, Lisl. LET'S GO TO THE MUSEUM. New York: Holiday House, 1989.

THE WORLD BOOK ENCYCLOPEDIA. Chicago: World Book, Inc., 1992.

Activity 1—Newspaper Business Terms
You will need: Pencil, paper, a book about the newspaper business.

Read a book about the newspaper business. Write the meanings of at least three of the following terms: dateline, dummy, deadline, morgue, headline, lead, editorial, paste-up, beat, edition, layout.

Activity 2—History of Newspapers
You will need: Pencil, paper, a book about the history of newspapers.

Read a book or a chapter about the history of newspapers. List at least four interesting facts that you learned from your reading.

Activity 3—"Five W's and the H"
You will need: Pencil, paper, a book about the job of a newspaper reporter.

Read a book about how reporters write newspaper stories. The "five w's and the h" are important to the work of reporters. On your paper explain what these letters mean and why they are important.

Activity 4—Newspaper Reporter
You will need: Pencil, paper, a book about the newspaper business.

Read a book about the newspaper business. Pretend that you are a reporter. Attend an event or happening in your town or school. Take accurate notes of what happens. Then write an article for a newspaper. Remember to include the "five w's and the h" in the first paragraph.

000–099
GENERALITIES:
JOURNALISM

Activity 5—Front Page News
You will need: Pencil, paper, a book about newspaper publishing.

Read a book about how the front page of a newspaper is arranged. Where are the important stories placed? Like a reporter, keep a notebook listing the things that happen in your school for one week. Decide which items are the most important. Make a layout of a front page using the events you've written about.

Activity 6—Television Reporter
You will need: Pencil, paper, a book about television reporting.

Read a book about being a television news reporter. Write a daily calendar for a day's work of a reporter. What will be done each hour of the day? Where will the reporter need to go? Who will the reporter be interviewing?

Activity 7—Columns & Feature Stories
You will need: Pencil, paper, a book about newspaper publishing.

Read a book about newspapers. List some of the many columns (Ann Landers, Dear Abby, etc.) and features (weather, comics, etc.) found in most newspapers.

Activity 8—Interviewing
You will need: Pencil, paper, a book about a reporter's job.

Read a book about the job of a reporter. Reporters often interview people to obtain information for a story. Pick a topic and pretend that you are interviewing someone. List ten questions that you would ask this person.

GENERALITIES:
JOURNALISM

Bly, Nellie. REPORTER FOR THE WORLD. Illus. by Martha E. Kendall. Brookfield, Connecticut: 1992.

Collins, Jean E. SHE WAS THERE: STORIES OF PIONEERING WOMEN JOURNALISTS. New York: Messner, 1980.

Craig, Janet. WHAT'S IT LIKE TO BE A NEWSPAPER REPORTER? Mahwah, New Jersey: Troll Assocs., 1989.

Crisman, Ruth. HOT OFF THE PRESS: GETTING THE NEWS INTO PRINT. Minneapolis: Lerner Pub., 1990.

Dahlstrom, Lorraine. WRITING DOWN THE DAYS: THREE HUNDRED SIXTY-FIVE CREATIVE JOURNALING IDEAS FOR YOUNG PEOPLE. Minneapolis: Free Spirit Pub., 1990.

Fenten, Don. BEHIND THE NEWSPAPER SCENE. Mankato, Minnesota: Crestwood House, 1980.

Fitz-Gerald, Christine. I CAN BE A REPORTER. Chicago: Childrens Press, 1986.

Fleming, Thomas. BEHIND THE HEADLINES. New York: Walker and Co., 1989.

Gibbons, Gail. DEADLINE! FROM NEWS TO NEWSPAPER. New York: Harper Collins, 1987.

Goldman, David. THE FREEDOM OF THE PRESS IN AMERICA. Minneapolis: Lerner Pub., 1968.

Jaspersohn, William. A DAY IN THE LIFE OF A TELEVISION NEWS REPORTER. Boston: Little, Brown, 1981.

Koral, April. IN THE NEWSROOM. New York: Watts, 1990.

Leedy, Loreen. THE FURRY NEWS: HOW TO MAKE A NEWSPAPER, New York: Holiday House, 1990.

Mabery, D. L. TELL ME ABOUT YOURSELF: HOW TO INTERVIEW ANYONE FROM YOUR FRIENDS TO FAMOUS PEOPLE. Minneapolis: Lerner Books, 1985.

Miller, Margaret. HOT OFF THE PRESS: A DAY AT THE DAILY NEWS. New York: Crown, 1985.

Petersen, David. NEWSPAPERS. Chicago: Childrens Press, 1983.

Trainer, David. A DAY IN THE LIFE OF A TV NEWS REPORTER. Photos by Stephen Sanacore. Mahwah, New Jersey: Troll Assoc., 1981.

Walters, Sarah. HOW NEWSPAPERS ARE MADE. New York: Facts on File, 1989.

Wolverton, Ruth and Mike Wolverton. THE NEWS MEDIA. New York: Watts, 1981.

Activity 1— Be Creative

You will need: Pencil, paper, books about creativity.

Read books about creativity. Write an activity that would help you and your friends learn something about creative thinking.

Activity 2—Problem Solving

You will need: Pencil, paper, books on problem solving or thinking.

Read books about problem solving or thinking. Then write at least three ways you learned to solve problems from the readings.

Activity 3—Dreams

You will need: Pencil, paper, a book about dreams.

Read a book or a chapter about dreams and dreaming. Do you usually remember your dreams? Are they pleasant? Frightening? Strange? Write a paragraph telling about one of your dreams.

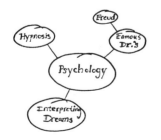

Activity 4—Webbing Information

You will need: Pencil, paper, a book relating to psychology.

Read a book relating to psychology. Then draw a web to show the important facts that you learned from your reading.

Activity 5—"ESP"
You will need: Pencil, paper, books on ESP.

Read books to learn about ESP. On your paper, explain what ESP is. Write one example of this mind-mystery.

Activity 6—Imagine
You will need: Pencil, paper, a book about imagination.

Read a book or a chapter on imagination. Imagine what it would be like to live on Mars. Then draw a picture of this scene.

Activity 7—Psychology—What is it?
You will need: Pencil, paper, books on psychology.

Read books about psychology. Think about what you have learned. Write about how at least two of the things you learned can help you.

Activity 8—Memory
You will need: Pencil, paper, a book on memory.

Read a book or a chapter about memory. Then list at least five ways that you can improve your own memory.

Activity 9—Optical Illusions
You will need: Pencil, paper, books on optical illusions.

Read books about optical illusions. Draw an example of an optical illusion.

PHILOSOPHY AND RELATED DISCIPLINES:
PSYCHOLOGY

Baldwin, Dorothy. HEALTH AND FEELINGS. Vero Beach, Florida: Rourke Enterprises, Inc., 1987.

Berry, Joy. EVERY KID'S GUIDE TO UNDERSTANDING NIGHTMARES. Illus. by Bartholemew. Chicago: Childrens Press, 1987.

Berger, Terry. FRIENDS. Photos by Alice Kandell. New York: Julian Messner, 1981.

Garner, Robert. EXPERIMENTING WITH ILLUSIONS. New York: Franklin Watts, 1990.

Gilbert, Sara. USING YOUR HEAD: THE MANY WAYS OF BEING SMART. New York: Macmillan Publishing Company, 1984.

Goley, Elaine. LEARN THE VALUE OF TRUST. Illus. by Debbie Crocker. Vero Beach, Florida: Rourke Enterprises, 1987.

Greenberg, Judith E. and Helen H. Carey. SUNNY: THE DEATH OF A PET. New York: Franklin Watts, 1986.

Kettelkamp, Larry. YOUR MARVELOUS MIND. Philadelphia: The Westminster Press, 1980.

Milios, R. SLEEPING AND DREAMING. Chicago: Childrens Press, 1987.

Moser, Adolph. DON'T POP YOUR CORK ON MONDAYS! Illus. by David Pilkey. Kansas City, Missouri: Landmark Editions, Inc. 1988.

Nozaki, Akihiro and Mitsumasa Anno. ANNO'S HAT TRICKS. New York: Philomel Books, 1985.

Orli, Eiji and Masako Orli. SIMPLE SCIENCE EXPERIMENTS WITH OPTICAL ILLUSIONS. Pictures by Kaoru Fujishima. Milwaukee, Wisconsin: Gareth Stevens, 1989.

Parker, Steve. DREAMING IN THE NIGHT: HOW YOU REST, SLEEP AND DREAM. New York: Watts, 1991.

Sternberg, Patricia. HOW TO PUT CONFIDENCE IN YOUR CONVERSATION. New York: Lathrop, Lee and Shepard, 1984.

Watson, Jane Werner, Robert E. Switzer and J. Cotter Hurschberg. SOMETIMES I'M AFRAID. Pictures by Irene Travas. New York: Crown Publishers, 1986.

White, Laurence B. Jr. and Ray Broekel. OPTICAL ILLUSIONS. New York: Franklin Watts, 1986.

Yepsen, Roger. SMARTEN UP!: HOW TO INCREASE YOUR BRAIN POWER. Boston: Little, Brown, 1990.

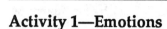

Activity 1—Emotions
You will need: Pencil, paper, books on human emotions.

Read books about human emotions. Define the word *emotion* in your own words. Make a picture about your favorite emotions.

Activity 2—Care About Others
You will need: Pencil, paper, books about caring.

Read books about caring. In complete sentences write at least six ways people can care about others.

Activity 3—Honesty
You will need: Pencil, paper, books about honesty.

Read books about honesty. Write how you feel when someone is honest and how you feel when someone is dishonest with you. Write at least three ways that you can be a more honest person.

Activity 4—Charting Emotions
You will need: Pencil, paper, books on human emotions.

Read books about the emotions that everyone feels. For at least one day, note the emotions that you experienced, what caused each emotion, and how you acted because of it. Make a chart of your experiences.

Example:

Emotion	Cause	Action
Anger	Someone called me a name.	I walked away from this person.

Activity 5—Different Emotions
You will need: Pencil, paper, books on human emotions.

Read about human emotions. List at least eight different kinds of emotions that we all feel. Underline the ones you have experienced.

Activity 6—Happiness
You will need: Pencil, paper, a book on joy or happiness.

Read a book about joy or happiness. Write the word *HAPPINESS* in the center of a large sheet of paper. Then draw pictures of things around this word that make you feel happy.

Activity 7—Friendship
You will need: Pencil, paper, books about friendship.

Read books about friends and friendship. Define friendship in your own words. Draw a picture of a time when you think you were being a good friend. Below your picture explain how you felt when you were being a good friend.

Activity 8—Comfortable/Uncomfortable
You will need: Pencil, paper, a book about human emotions.

Read a book about human emotions. List these emotions on a chart under the headings of *Comfortable* and *Uncomfortable*.

Comfortable	Uncomfortable

PHILOSOPHY AND RELATED DISCIPLINES:
PSYCHOLOGY (EMOTIONS)

Anderson, Penny S. ANGRY. Milwaukee, Wisconsin: Raintree, 1991.

Berry, Joy. EVERY KID'S GUIDE TO BEING SPECIAL. Illus. by Bartholomew. Chicago: Childrens Press, 1987.

Berry, Joy. EVERY KID'S GUIDE TO DECISION MAKING AND PROBLEM SOLVING. Illus. by Bartholomew. Chicago: Childrens Press, 1987.

Berry, Joy. EVERY KID'S GUIDE TO HANDLING DISAGREEMENTS. Chicago: Childrens Press, 1987.

Berry, Joy. EVERY KID'S GUIDE TO HANDLING FEELINGS. Illus. by Bartholomew. Chicago: Childrens Press, 1987.

Berry, Joy. EVERY KID'S GUIDE TO MAKING FRIENDS. Illus. by Bartholomew. Chicago: Childrens Press, 1987.

Barsuhn, Rochelle N. FEELING ANGRY. Illus. by Kathryn Hutton. Mankato, Minnesota: Child's World, 1983.

Dombrower, Jan. GETTING TO KNOW YOUR FEELINGS. Illus. by Patricia Stricklin. Pleasanton, California: Heartwise Press, 1990.

Goldman, Margaret F. MY A, B, C, D, E THINKING, FEELING AND DOING BOOK. Illus. by Diane Era. Apple Valley, California: L & M Books, 1989.

Goley, Elaine P. LEARN THE VALUE OF FRIENDSHIP. Illus. by Debbie Crocker. Vero Beach, Florida: Rourke, 1987.

Goley, Elaine P. LEARN THE VALUE OF HONESTY. Illus. by Debbie Crocker. Vero Beach, Florida: Rourke, 1987.

Goley, Elaine P. LEARN THE VALUE OF JOY. Illus. by Debbie Crocker. Vero Beach, Florida: Rourke, 1993.

Goley, Elaine P. LEARN THE VALUE OF SELF CONTROL. Illus. by Debbie Crocker. Vero Beach, Florida: Rourke, 1993.

Goley, Elaine P. LEARN THE VALUE OF TRUST. Illus. by Debbie Crocker. Vero Beach, Florida: Rourke, 1987.

Hazen, Barbara S. WHAT ARE FEELINGS? Illus. by Lynn Sweat. Lake Forest, IL: Forest House, 1990.

Odor, Ruth S. MOODS AND EMOTIONS. Illus. by John Bolt. Mankato, Minnesota: Child's World, 1980.

200–299
RELIGION:
RELIGIONS

Activity 1—Religions of the World
You will need: Pencil, paper, books about different religions.

Read about various religions of the world. List at least six different religions.

Activity 2—Places of Worship
You will need: Pencil, paper, a book about places of religious worship.

Read about a place of worship that is different from where you might worship. Illustrate and label this place of worship.

Activity 3—Religious Freedom
You will need: Pencil, paper, a book about religious freedom.

What is the First Amendment to the Constitution? Why was it written? Do you agree with it? Explain your answer in writing.

Activity 4—Religious Celebrations
You will need: Pencil, paper, a book about religious holidays.

Read about a religious holiday or special celebration. Write a paragraph and make a picture about it.

Activity 5—Sacred Laws
You will need: Pencil, paper, books about religious laws.

Many religions follow specific laws that are written into sacred books. Choose a religion and write at least three of its laws.

200–299
RELIGION:
RELIGIONS

Activity 6—Religious Locations
You will need: Pencil, paper, books about religious places.

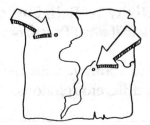

Name at least two important religious locations in the world. Write why these places are important. Locate them on a map.

Activity 7—Religious Figures
You will need: Pencil, paper, books about historical religious figures.

List at least three religious figures of the past. Tell who they were and what important things they did.

Activity 8—Religious Symbols
You will need: Pencil, crayons, drawing paper, books about religions.

Read about religious symbols. Draw, label, and color at least three of them on a sheet of drawing paper.

Activity 9—Researching Religions of the World
You will need: Pencil, paper, a book about religions of the world.

Read a book that relates to religions of the world. Write at least six interesting facts that you learned from your reading.

Activity 10—Religion Picture Book
You will need: Pencil, crayons, paper, books about religion.

Pick a religion that interests you. Make a glossar/picture book with words and pictures (symbols) that relate to the religion you chose.

RELIGION:
RELIGIONS

Ahsan, M. M. MUSLIM FESTIVALS. Vero Beach, Florida: Rourke Corp., 1987.

Berger, Gilda. RELIGIONS: A REFERENCE FIRST BOOK. Milwaukee, Wisconsin: Gareth Stevens, 1991.

Chaikim, Miriam. MENORAHS, MEZUZAS, AND OTHER JEWISH SYMBOLS. Illus. by Erika Weihs. Miamisburg, Ohio: Clarion Books, 1990.

Domnitz, Meyer. JUDAISM. New York: Bookwright Press, 1986.

Edmonds, I.G. BUDDHISM: A FIRST BOOK. New York: Watts, 1978.

Hood, Abdul Latif Al. ISLAM. New York: Bookwright Press, 1987.

Kanitkar, V. P. HINDUISM. New York: Bookwright Press, 1986.

Kettlelkamp, Larry. RELIGIONS, EAST AND WEST. New York: William Morrow , 1972.

Krause, Father Joseph E. A CHILDREN'S BIBLE. New York: Golden Press, 1962.

Lathrop, Dorothy, P. ANIMALS OF THE BIBLE. New York: HarperCollins, 1965.

Lerner, Carol. A BIBLICAL GARDEN. New York: William Morrow and Company, 1982.

Makhlouf, Georgia. THE RISE OF MAJOR RELIGIONS. Illus. by Michael Welply. Englewood Cliffs, New Jersey: Silver Burdett Press, 1986.

McCaughrean, Geraldine. THE STORY OF NOAH AND THE ARK. Nashville, Tennessee: Ideals Children's Books, 1989.

Miller, Calvin. BUCKETS OF NOTHING: THE STORY OF CREATION IN RHYME. Nashville, Tennessee: Thomas Nelson Publishers, 1987.

NOAH'S ARK. New York: Dutton Children's Books, 1990.

Raghaveshananda, Swami. STORY OF SRI KRISHNA FOR CHILDREN. Hollywood, California: Vendata Pr., 1990.

Snelling, John. BUDDHISM. New York: Bookwright Press, 1986.

Thomas, M. and Mary L. Ramey. MANY CHILDREN: RELIGIONS AROUND THE WORLD. Illus. by Patti L. Lucas. Reston, Virginia: M. A. Thomas, 1987.

Underwood, Lynn. RELIGION AND SOCIETY. Milwaukee, Wisconsin: Gareth Stevens, 1991.

Ward, Hiley H. MY FRIEND'S BELIEFS. New York: Walker and Co., 1988.

200-299
RELIGION: MYTHS

Activity 1—Read and Write a Myth

You will need: Pencil, paper, a book of myths.

Although no one really knows how or why myths were created, many people who study them believe that they were written to explain things in nature that people did not understand. Read a myth that explains some natural happening. Then write a myth of your own to explain some natural happening.

Activity 2—Illustrate Your Favorite Myth

You will need: Pencil, crayons/markers, paper, a book of myths.

Read about three or more different myths. Illustrate some part of your favorite myth. Write a paragraph explaining your illustration. (Be sure to write the title of the myth above your illustration.)

Activity 3—Myths to Explain Events

You will need: Pencil, paper, books about myths.

Read two different myths that explain the same event. Write a paragraph explaining how the myths are alike and how they are different.

Activity 4—Characters in a Myth

You will need: Pencil, paper, a book of myths

Read at least two myths. Choose the one that you like best. On your paper list at least three characters. Write a two or three sentence description of each one. Name the characters, describe the characters' appearance, and tell what each character is like.

Activity 5—Perform A Myth
You will need: Pencil, paper, a book of myths.

Read two or more myths. Choose one and rewrite it as a play. You and some of your classmates might wish to perform the play for others.

Activity 6—Rewrite a Myth
You will need: Pencil, paper, a book of myths.

Myths of long ago have often been retold many times by many different authors. Read two myths. Choose the one that you like better and rewrite it in simpler language so that a young child could understand and enjoy it.

Activity 7—Setting of a Myth
You will need: Pencil, paper, a book of myths.

Look up the word *setting.* Write a definition of the word's meaning as it relates to a story or a play. Myths often have strange or imaginative settings. Read at least two myths. Choose the one that you like better. Draw a picture to show the setting of the story.

Activity 8—Make a List of Myths
You will need: Pencil, paper, books of myths.

Make a list of titles of books of myths that you have found. Include the title, author, place of publication, publisher, and publication date. Give yourself one point for each book title you record, and five points for each book you read.

TOTAL POINTS:

RELIGION:
MYTHS

Asimov, Isaac. MYTHOLOGY AND THE UNIVERSE. Milwaukee, Wisconsin: Gareth Stevens, 1989.

Baskin, Hosie and Leonard Baskin. A BOOK OF DRAGONS. Illus. by Leonard Baskin. New York: Knopf/Borzoi, 1985.

Campbell, Joseph. THE POWER OF MYTHS. New York: Doubleday, 1988.

Climo, Shirley. KING OF THE BIRDS. Illus. by Ruth Heller. New York: Crowell, 1988.

Fisher, Leonard Everett. CYCLOPS. New York: Holiday House, 1991.

Fisher, Leonard Everett. (retold) THESEUS AND THE MINOTAUR. New York: Holiday House, 1988.

Gerstein, Mordicai. TALES OF PAN. New York: Harper and Row, 1986.

Goble, Paul. THE GREAT RACE OF THE BIRDS AND ANIMALS. New York: Bradbury, 1985.

Graves, Robert. GREEK GODS AND HEROES. New York: Dell, 1965.

Hamilton, Virginia. IN THE BEGINNING: CREATION STORIES FROM AROUND THE WORLD. Illus. by Barry Moser. New York: Harcourt Brace Jovanovich, 1988.

HEART OF GOLD. Illus. by Rosalyn White. Oakland, California: Dharma Publishing, 1989.

Jaffrey, Madhur. SEASONS OF SPLENDOR: TALES, MYTHS AND LEGENDS OF INDIA. Illus. by Michael Foreman. New York: Atheneum, 1985.

Lattimore, Deborah N. THE PRINCE AND THE GOLDEN AX: A MINOAN TALE. Illus. by author. New York: HarperCollins Child Books, 1988.

Low, Alice. THE MACMILLAN BOOK OF GREEK GODS AND HEROS. Illus. by Arvis Stewart. New York: Macmillan, 1985.

Monroe, Jean G., and Ray A. Williamson. THEY DANCE IN THE SKY: NATIVE AMERICAN STAR MYTHS. Illus. by Edgar Stewart. New York: Houghton Mifflin, 1987.

Osborne, Mary Pope. FAVORITE GREEK MYTHS. New York: Scholastic Inc., 1989.

Osborne, Mary Pope. PANDORA'S BOX. Illus. by Lasa Amoroso. New York: Scholastic/Hello Reader Books, 1987.

THE RABBIT IN THE MOON. Illus. by Rosalyn White. Oakland, California: Dharma Publishing, 1989.

Weil, Lisl. PANDORA'S BOX. New York: Atheneum, 1986.

300–399
SOCIAL SCIENCES:
FAIRY TALES AND FOLK TALES

Activity 1—Words From a Tale
You will need: Pencil, paper, a book of fairy tales or folk tales.

Read a tale that you have never read before. List at least ten names, words, or phrases that come to mind when you think about this story.

Activity 2—My Favorite Tale
You will need: Pencil, paper, a book of fairy tales or folk tales.

Read three or more tales. Make a list of those you read. Which is your favorite one? Tell why you like it best.

Activity 3—Illustrate Your Favorite Tale
You will need: Pencil, crayons/markers, paper, a book of fairy tales or folk tales.

Reread your favorite tale. Draw a picture of your favorite scene from the story. Write the name of the tale beneath your drawing. On the back of your paper, write a paragraph telling why this is your favorite scene.

Activity 4—Shape Picture
You will need: Pencil, crayons/markers, scissors, large sheet of construction paper, a book of fairy tales or folk tales.

Reread a tale that you like. Choose an object that relates to the story, for example; a shoe from the story, "The Shoemaker and the Elves." On a sheet of construction paper, draw the shape as large as you can. Cut out the shape. Make an illustration of a scene from the story on the shape. Write the title of the tale somewhere on the shape.

Activity 5—The Three Bears
You will need: Pencil, crayons, paper, a book of "The Three Bears."

Read the tale, "The Three Bears." On your paper, draw and label three like objects that are in the story. For example, you could draw three bowls: Baby Bear's bowl, Mama Bear's bowl, and Papa Bear's bowl.

Activity 6—Same Story, Different Countries
You will need: Pencil, paper, a book of fairy tales from other countries.

Read a familiar fairy tale. Then read the same tale as written from a different culture. Explain how these tales are similar and different.

Activity 7—Same Story, Different Authors
You will need: Pencil, paper, books of fairy tales or folk tales.

The same fairy tale is often retold by different authors. In various retellings you will find some differences in the same story. Read two versions of the same tale. Write at least one paragraph about how the stories are similar and at least one paragraph about how they are different.

Activity 8—Webbing a New Tale
You will need: Pencil, paper, a book of fairy tales or folk tales.

Read a tale that you have not read before. Draw a web as seen in the illustration at left. Write the title of the story in the center, then add highlights from the tale on the lines that extend from the center.

SOCIAL SCIENCES:
FAIRY TALES AND FOLK TALES

Andersen, Hans Christian. THE WILD SWANS. Illus. by Susan Jeffers. New York: Puffin, 1981.

Botkin, B. A., ed. A TREASURY OF AMERICAN FOLKLORE. New York: Bonanza, 1983.

Calvino, Italo. ITALIAN FOLKTALES. New York: Harcourt Brace Jovanovich, 1980.

Clarkson, Atelia, and Gilbert B. Cross. WORLD FOLKTALES. New York: Scribner, 1980.

Cole, Joanna. BEST LOVED FOLK TALES OF THE WORLD. Illus. by Jill Karla Schwarz. New York: Anchor, 1982.

Collins, Megan. THE WILLOW MAIDEN. Illus. by Laszlo Gal. New York: Dial/Pied Piper, 1988.

Crossley-Holland, Kevin, ed, BRITISH FOLK TALES. Illus. by Bert Dodson. New York: Orchard, 1987.

Cushing, Frank Hamilton. ZUNI FOLK TALES. Tucson, Arizona: University of Arizona Press, 1986.

Eisen, Armand. GOLDILOCKS AND THE THREE BEARS. Illus. by Lynn Bywaters Ferris. New York: Knopf/Borzoi, 1987.

FAVORITE TALES OF HANS CHRISTIAN ANDERSEN. New York: Checkerboard, 1988.

Hamilton, Virginia. THE EPOPLE COULD FLY: AMERICAN BLACK FOLKTALES. Illus. by Leo Dillon and Diane Dillon. New York: Knopf, 1985.

Hodges, Margaret. SAINT GEORGE AND THE DRAGON: A GOLDEN LEGEND. Illus. by Trina Schart Hyman. Boston: Little, Brown, 1984.

Lester, Julius. THE TALES OF UNCLE REMUS: THE ADVENTURES OF BRER RABBIT. Illus. by Jerry Pinkney. New York: Dial, 1987.

Manheim, Ralph. GRIMM'S TALES FOR YOUNG AND OLD: THE COMPLETE STORIES. New York: Doubleday, 1983.

Marshall, James. GOLDILOCKS AND THE THREE BEARS. New York: Dial, 1988.

Perrault, Charles. CINDERELLA. Illus. by Marcia Brown. New York: Macmillan, 1988.

Rogasky, Barbara. THE WATER OF LIFE: A TALE FROM THE BROTHERS GRIMM. Illus. by Trina Schart Hyman. New York: Holiday House, 1986.

Scieszka, Jon. THE TRUE STORY OF THE THREE LITTLE PIGS. Illus. by Lane Smith. New York: Viking-Kestrel, 1989.

Yolen, Jane, ed. FAVORITE FOLKTALES FROM AROUND THE WORLD. New York: Pantheon, 1986.

300–399
SOCIAL SCIENCES:
THE EARTH (ENVIRONMENT)

Activity 1—Environmental Newspaper Article
You will need: Pencil, paper, books about environmental problems.

Locate information about something that you consider to be an environmental problem. Then pretend you are writing an editorial for a newspaper. Describe the problem, give reasons why you consider it a problem, and try to persuade readers to do what is necessary to either improve the situation or eliminate the problem.

Activity 2—Research Recycling Problems
You will need: Pencil, paper, books about recycling.

Research various types of materials which are thrown away each year in North America. Using this information, write about three recycling problems. Suggest solutions to these problems. You might find it fun to trade problems and solve those another student discovered.

Activity 3—Save the Earth
You will need: Pencil, paper, books about the environment.

Research ways that people can save the earth. List ten things that you can do to help improve the environment.

Activity 4—Recycle Newspapers
You will need: Marker, large paper grocery bag, books about recycling.

Read a book about recycling. Write the words <u>Recycled Newspapers</u> on a large paper bag. Decorate the bag with pictures that relate to recycling. Use the bag to collect folded newspapers to be taken to a recycling center or collection point.

300–399
SOCIAL SCIENCES:
THE EARTH (ENVIRONMENT)

Activity 5—Keeping the Earth Healthy

You will need: Pencil, crayons/markers, a large piece of tagboard or heavy paper, a book about the environment.

Read a book to learn about keeping the earth healthy. Make a poster to promote the idea. Get permission to display your poster.

Activity 6—Environmental Agencies

You will need: Pencil, paper, envelope, books about the environment.

Read books about the environment. Many such books provide names and addresses of environmental agencies. Write to one of these agencies and ask about ways that you can help preserve and improve the environment. Share the information with the class.

Activity 7—Environmental Vocabulary

You will need: Pencil, paper, books about the environment.

Choose at least six words or phrases from the following list: environment, pollution, recycle, landfill, ozone layer, acid rain, conservation, endangered species, litter. Research the meanings of these words. On your paper, define the words and use each word in a sentence.

Activity 8—Environmental Research

You will need: Pencil, paper, a book about the environment.

Research an experiment relating to the environment. Do the experiment at home or in school. Write an account of the experiment and your observations. Share the results with your class.

SOCIAL SCIENCES
THE EARTH (ENVIRONMENT)

Baines, Chris. THE PICNIC: AN ECOLOGY STORY BOOK. New York: Interlink Pub., 1990.

Bellamy, David. HOW GREEN ARE YOU? New York: Crown, 1991.

BLUE AND BEAUTIFUL: PLANET EARTH, OUR HOME. New York: UN, 1990.

Brumley, Karen. SAVING OUR PLANET. Illus. by Tammy Altop. Columbus, Ohio: American Education Pub., 1991.

Dehr, Roma and Ronald Bazar. GOOD PLANETS ARE HARD TO FIND: AN ENVIRONMENTAL INFORMATION GUIDE FOR KIDS. Illus. by Nola Johnson. Buffalo, New York: Firefly Books Ltd., 1990.

Diffenderfer, Susan. ECOLOGY: LEARNING TO LOVE OUR PLANET. Tuscon, Arizona: Zephyr Press, 1984.

Earth Works Project staff. FIFTY SIMPLE THINGS YOU CAN DO TO SAVE THE EARTH. Alahambra, California: Greenleaf Pub., 1990.

Elkington, John GOING GREEN: A KID'S HANDBOOK TO SAVING THE PLANET. Illus. by Tony Ross. New York: Puffin Books, 1990.

Flora, Sherrill. TREAT THE EARTH GENTLY. Minneapolis, Minnesota: T.S. Denison, 1991.

Greene, Carol. CARING FOR OUR AIR. Hillside, New Jersey: Enslow, 1991.

Greene, Carol. CARING FOR OUR LAND. Hillside, New Jersey: Enslow, 1991.

Hare, Tony. VANISHING HABITATS. New York: Watts, 1991.

Herridge, Douglas and Susan Hughes. THE ENVIRONMENTAL DETECTIVE KIT. New York: HarperCollins Child Books, 1991.

Norsgaard, E. Jaediker. NATURE'S GREAT BALANCING ACT: IN OUR OWN BACKYARD. New York: Dutton Child Books, 1990.

Rosney, Birde, ed. NATURE IN ACTION: YOUNG READERS ECOLOGY HANDBOOK. Chester Park, Pennsylvania: Dufour, 1978.

Schwartz, Linda. EARTH BOOK FOR KIDS: ACTIVITIES TO HELP HEAL THE ENVIRONMENT. Illus. by Beverly Armstrong. Santa Barbara, California: Learning Works, 1990.

Stone, L. DESERTS. Vero Beach, Florida: Rourke Corp., 1989.

Stone, L. PRAIRIES. Vero Beach, Florida: Rourke Corp., 1989.

Stone, L. RAIN FORESTS. Vero Beach, Florida: Rourke Corp., 1989.

Yanda, Bill. RADS, ERGS AND CHEESEBURGERS: THE KID'S GUIDE TO ENERGY AND THE ENVIRONMENT. New York: John Muir, 1991.

400–499
Language:
Dictionaries

Activity 1—Nonsense Words
You will need: Pencil, paper, dictionary.

Each entry in a dictionary is divided into syllables. Following each entry you will find a phonetic respelling of the word to help you pronounce the word correctly. Study this nonsense word: <u>bromdelunk</u>. Divide the word into syllables and write a phonetic respelling of it. Refer to the pronunciation key in a dictionary to help you. What do you think this nonsense word could mean? Write a definition. Now make up two or more nonsense words of your own. Divide each word into syllables and write your own phonetic respellings along with a definition for each word.

Activity 2—Defining Shapes
You will need: Pencil, paper, dictionary.

Use a dictionary to define the words *angle* and *parallel*. On your paper draw examples to show the meanings of the words. Label the illustrations. Look up and draw illustrations of the following shapes: octagon, trapezoid, hexagon, triangle. Label each illustration.

Activity 3—Famous People
You will need: Pencil, paper, dictionary.

Look up the names of at least three famous people. Write two or more facts about each person. You may need to use more than one dictionary. (Hint: *Most dictionaries have a biographical section in the back.*)

Activity 4—Syllables
You will need: Pencil, paper, dictionary.

Find and write at least ten words that have more than three syllables. Divide these words into syllables as seen in the dictionary.

Activity 5—Dictionaries and Geographical Locations
You will need: Pencil, paper, dictionary, map.

Look up the names of five large cities. Write the names and locations of the cities on your paper. Put a star by each one that you locate on a map. (Hint: *Most dictionaries have a geographical section in the back.*)

Activity 6—Specialized Dictionaries
You will need: Pencil, paper, dictionary of special terms and words.

Look at a dictionary that specializes in a specific area, subject, or occupation. Using this dictionary, create an interesting activity such as a game, worksheet, report, or art project.

Activity 7—Picture Dictionary
You will need: Pencil, crayons/markers, booklet or spiral notebook, old magazines, scissors, glue, picture dictionary.

Study a picture dictionary. Then create your own picture dictionary. Find or draw pictures that begin with each letter of the alphabet. Cut out the pictures. Print the letters of the alphabet neatly on separate sheets of paper. Glue the correct pictures to the correct pages.

Activity 8—Music Dictionary
You will need: Pencil, paper, music dictionary.

Anyone who sings a song from a songbook will need to know many common musical terms and symbols. Using a music dictionary, define the following terms: rest, crescendo, decrescendo, diminuendo, acapella, adagio, allegretto, piano, pianissimo, largo, and accelerando. If a symbol is listed for the term, draw it on your paper.

LANGUAGE:
DICTIONARIES

Eastman, P. K. CAT IN THE HAT BEGINNER BOOK DICTIONARY. New York: Beginner Books, 1964.

FIRST PICTURE DICTIONARY. New York: Outlet Books, 1985.

Greisman, Joan. FIRST DICTIONARY. New York: Western Pub., 1990.

THE LINCOLN DICTIONARY FOR CHILDREN: THE DICTIONARY FOR WRITING. Milwaukee, Wisconsin: Raintree Pubs., 1988.

THE LINCOLN WRITING DICTIONARY FOR CHILDREN. San Diego, California: Harcourt Brace, Jovanovich 1988.

THE MACMILLAN DICTIONARY FOR CHILDREN. New York: Macmillan ChildGroup, 1989.

MY FIRST DICTIONARY. Chicago: Scott Foresman, 1989.

MY FIRST PICTURE DICTIONARY. New York: Outlet Books, 1985.

Schulz, Charles M. THE CHARLIE BROWN DICTIONARY. New York: Random, 1974.

Scott, Foresman. MY FIRST DICTIONARY. New York: HarperCollins, 1990.

Scott, Foresman. WORDS FOR NEW READERS. New York: HarperCollins, 1990.

SECOND PICTURE DICTIONARY. Auburn, Maine: Ladybird Books, 1980.

Snow, Alan. MY FIRST DICTIONARY. New York: Smithmark, 1991.

Steinberg, Margery A. DICTIONARY AND WORD SKILLS. New York: Putnam Group, 1979.

Stockley, C. DICTIONARY OF BIOLOGY: THE FACTS YOU NEED TO KNOW AT A GLANCE. Tulsa, Oklahoma: E.D.C., 1987.

Stockley, C. DICTIONARY OF PHYSICS: THE FACTS YOU NEED TO KNOW AT A GLANCE. Tulsa, Oklahoma: E.D.C., 1988.

Walt Disney Staff. MY FIRST MUPPET DICTIONARY. Burbank, California: W. Disney Pub., 1991.

WEBSTER'S NEW WORLD DICTIONARY FOR YOUNG READERS. New York: Simon and Schuster, 1989.

THE WEBSTER'S II NEW RIVERSIDE CHILDREN'S DICTIONARY. Boston: Houghton Mifflin, 1985.

Wittels, Harriet & Joan Greisman. THE CLEAR & SIMPLE THESAURUS DICTIONARY. New York: Putnam Pub. Group, 1976.

400–499
Language:
Foreign Language

Activity 1—Foreign Language Dictionary
You will need: Pencil, paper, foreign language dictionaries or phrase books.

Study books of foreign languages. Write down and learn to say the following words and phrases in at least two languages other than your own: please, thank you, yes, no, small, mother, father, teacher, bus.

Activity 2—Foreign Language Poetry
You will need: Pencil, paper, a book of poetry in a foreign language.

Find a short poem in a foreign language. Write it down. Try to find an English translation of the poem and write it on your paper.

Activity 3—French & Spanish
You will need: Pencil, paper, foreign language dictionaries or phrase books.

Several languages such as French and Spanish are known as Romance languages. Why are they called this? Since these languages have a common source, many of their words are similar. Find and list at least three words that are similar in two of the Romance languages.

Activity 4—Foreign Songs
You will need: Pencil, paper, a foreign language songbook.

Find a short song written in a foreign language. Copy the words of the song. If you can, find a translation and write the words out in English. Sing the words in both languages.

Activity 5—Chinese/Japanese Written Language
You will need: Pencil, paper, a book about the Chinese or Japanese languages.

Some written languages do not use letters of an alphabet, but instead use picture-like symbols called "characters." Read a book on a Japanese or Chinese language. Write three interesting facts that you learned. Find written samples of Chinese or Japanese. Copy the characters for one or more words or phrases. Label each character with its meaning.

Activity 6—Idioms
You will need: Pencil, paper, a book or chapter about idioms.

Read a book about idioms. What is an idiom? List three idioms that are new to you and explain what they mean. Write a sentence using each idiom.

Activity 7—History of a Language
You will need: Pencil, paper, a book about the history of a language.

Read a book about the history of a specific language. Write three new facts that you learned from your reading.

Activity 8—Foreign Languages of Your Choice
You will need: Pencil, paper, a book about a foreign language.

Read a book on a foreign language of your choice. Draw pictures of various objects and label each in the foreign language and in your own language.

LANGUAGE:
FOREIGN LANGUAGE

Amery, Heather and P. Di Bello. THE FIRST THOUSAND WORDS IN ITALIAN. Illus. by Stephen Cartwright. Tulsa, Oklahoma: EDC, 1983.

Amery, Heather and Katrina Kirilenko. THE FIRST THOUSAND WORDS IN RUSSIAN. Illus. by Stephen Cartwright. London: Usborne, 1983.

Bahan, Ben and Joe Dannis. SIGNS FOR ME: BASIC SIGN VOCABULARY FOR CHILDREN. Berkeley, California: Dawn Sign Press, 1990.

Bove, Linda. SIGN LANGUAGE ABC WITH LINDA BOVE. Illus. by Tom Cooke. Photographs by Anita and Steve Shevett. New York: Random House, 1985.

Brunhoff, Laurent de. BABAR'S FRENCH LESSONS. New York: Random House, 1963.

A CHILD'S PICTURE ENGLISH-JAPANESE DICTIONARY. New York: Adama Pubs Inc., 1987.

A CHILD'S PICTURE HEBREW DICTIONARY. Illus. by Ita Meshi. New York: Adama Books, 1985.

Farris, Katherine. THE KIDS CAN PRESS FRENCH AND ENGLISH WORD BOOK. Toronto, OH: Kids Can Press, Ltd., 1991.

Feelings, Muriel. JAMBO MEANS HELLO: SWAHILI ALPHABET BOOK. Illus. by Tom Feelings. New York: Dial Press, 1974.

Flodin, Mickey. SIGNING FOR KIDS: THE FUN WAY FOR ANYONE TO LEARN AMERICAN SIGN LANGUAGE. New York: Putnam Publishing Group, 1991.

Haskins, Jim. COUNT YOUR WAY THROUGH GERMANY. Illus. by Helen Byers. Minneapolis: Carolrhoda, 1991.

Haskins, Jim. COUNT YOUR WAY THROUGH ITALY. Illus. by Beth Wright. Minneapolis: Carolrhoda, 1990.

Marsh, Carole. LATIN FOR KIDS: OF ALL THE GAUL. Decatur, Georgia: Gallopade Pub. Group, 1983.

Postman, Frederica. THE YIDDISH ALPHABET BOOK. Illus. by Bonnie Stone. New York: Adama Books, 1988.

Wiese, Kurt. YOU CAN WRITE CHINESE. New York: Viking, 1973.

Wikes, Angela. PASSPORT'S LANGUAGE GUIDE: ITALIAN FOR BEGINNERS. Illus. by John Shackell. Chicago: National Textbook Co., 1988.

Wikes, Angela. PASSPORT'S LANGUAGE GUIDE: SPANISH FOR BEGINNERS. Chicago: National Textbook Co., 1987.

Wikes, Angela. SPANISH PICTURE DICTIONARY. Chicago: National Textbook Co., 1988.

500–599
PURE SCIENCES: BOTANY (TREES)

Activity 1—Paragraph About a Tree
You will need: Pencil, paper, a book about different kinds of trees.

Read a book about different kinds of trees. Write a paragraph describing one or more of them.

Activity 2—Read, then Draw a Tree
You will need: Pencil, crayons, paper, a book about trees.

Read a book about trees and draw a picture of your favorite kind.

Activity 3—Bibliography of Tree Books
You will need: Pencil, paper, books about trees.

Make a bibliography of the books that are available on trees. Include the name of the author, the book title, the place of the publication, the publisher, and the publication date. Draw a small tree beside the books that you have read.

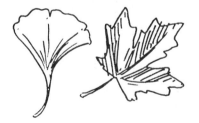

Activity 4—Read About Specific Trees
You will need: Pencil, crayons, paper, books about trees.

Read about the following trees: oak, apple, birch, maple, spruce, elm. Draw and label a picture of a leaf from each tree.

Activity 5—What Comes From Trees?
You will need: Pencil, paper, books about trees.

Read to discover what comes from trees. List at least ten products from trees.

Activity 6—Orchards
You will need: Pencil, paper, a book about fruit trees.

An orchard is a field of fruit trees. Read a book that tells about orchards. What kind of orchards did you read about? Write a paragraph about an orchard. Draw a picture of an orchard you would like to have. You might want to include yourself in the picture.

Activity 7—Planting a Tree
You will need: Pencil, paper, books about planting trees.

Read to discover the proper way of planting a tree. Draw several illustrations showing the steps of planting a tree. Write a caption below each picture.

Activity 8—Trees and Changing Seasons
You will need: Pencil, crayons, paper, books about trees through the seasons.

Read books about how trees change with the seasons. Fold a piece of paper into fourths. Draw a tree in each section of the paper to show how it looks during each season. Write the name of the season in each section.

Activity —Label Tree Parts
You will need: Pencil, paper, a book about various trees.

Read about a tree that you have never seen. Draw and label its parts, then write a description of it. Make your description as detailed as possible so that a person who is reading it will know what the tree looks like.

PURE SCIENCES:
BOTANY (TREES)

Adler, David A. REDWOODS ARE THE TALLEST TREES IN THE WORLD. Illus. by Kazue Mizumura. New York: Thomas Y. Crowell, 1978.

Bash, Barbara. TREE OF LIFE: THE WORLD OF THE AFRICAN BAOBAB. San Francisco, California: Sierra Club, 1989.

Boulton, Carolyn. TREES. Illus. by Colin Newman. New York: Franklin Watts, 1984.

Brandt, Keith. DISCOVERING TREES. Illus. by Christine W. Nigoghossian. Mahwah, New Jersey: Troll Assoc., 1982.

Burnie, David. TREE. Photos by Peter Chadwick. New York: Alfred A. Knopf, 1988.

Cochrane, Jennifer. TREES OF THE TROPICS. Austin, Texas: Steck-V, 1990.

Dickinson, Jane. ALL ABOUT TREES. Illus. by Anthony D'Adamo. Mahwah, New Jersey: Troll Assoc., 1983.

Fischer-Nagel, Heiderose and Andreas Fischer-Nagel. FIR TREES. Minneapolis, Minnesota: Carolrhoda, 1989.

Garelick, May and Barbara Brenner. THE TREMENDOUS TREE BOOK. Illus. by Fred Brenner. New York: Four Winds Press, 1979.

Greenaway, Theresa. WOODLAND TREES (series). Austin, Texas: Steck-Vaughn,1991.

Harlow, Rosie and Morgan Gareth. TREES AND LEAVES. Illus. by Liz Peperell. New York: Franklin Watts, 1991

Hester, Nigel. THE LIVING TREE. New York: Franklin Watts, 1990.

Hiscock, Bruce. THE BIG TREE. Illus. by Bruce Hiscock. New York: Macmillan Child Group, 1991

Kirkpatrick, Rena K. LOOK AT TREES. Illus. by Jo Worth and Ann Knight. Milwaukee, Wisconsin: Raintree Pub., 1985.

Langley, Andrew. TREES. New York: Franklin Watts, 1988.

Mitgutsch, Ali. FROM TREE TO TABLE. Minneapolis, Minnesota: Carolrhoda, 1971.

Podendorf, Illa. TREES. Chicago: Childrens Press. 1982.

Selsam, Millicent E. TREE FLOWERS. Illus. by Carol Lerner. New York: William Morrow, 1984.

Watts, Barrie. APPLE TREE. Morristown, New Jersey: Silver Burdett, 1987.

500–599
PURE SCIENCES: ASTRONOMY

Activity 1—The Moon
You will need: Pencil, paper, a book about the moon.

The moon goes through phases, or cycles—a pattern of changes repeated over and over. Find a book about the moon that shows illustrations of the phases of the moon. Draw pictures of the moon phases. Label the phases.

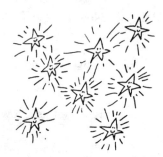

Activity 2—The Stars
You will need: Pencil, paper, books about the stars.

Read two or more books about the stars. On your paper, list six interesting facts that you learned from your readings.

Activity 3—The Sun
You will need: Pencil, crayons/markers, paper, a book about the sun.

Read a book about the sun. Decide which part of the book you liked best. Make an illustration of your favorite part of the book. Write a paragraph to describe your picture.

Activity 4—Questions About Astronomy
You will need: Pencil, paper, books about astronomy.

Write at least six questions about astronomy that you would like to have answered. Using the astronomy books, discover and write answers to as many of the questions as possible.

 500–599
PURE SCIENCES:
ASTRONOMY

Activity 5—A Play About Astronomy
You will need: Pencil, paper, a book about astronomy.

Read a book on astronomy. Then write a play that relates
to the information you discovered through your reading.

Activity 6—Write a Book Jacket Blurb
*You will need: Pencil, paper, books that have book jackets, a book
relating to astronomy.*

Many hardcover books come with removable paper cov-
ers called book jackets. The front inside flap of a book
Jacket usually has a blurb about the book. This functions
as advertisement for the book and gives information
about the story or content of the book and tells how the
book will help or interest the reader. Study the book jacket
blurbs on several books. Read a book about astronomy.
Write a book jacket blurb about the book. Tell why the
book is special and will be important to the reader.

Activity 7—The Planets
You will need: Pencil, paper, books about the planets.

Read two books about one or more planets. On your
paper, write the titles of the two books. Draw a star by the
title of the book that you like best. Then write one or more
paragraphs explaining the reasons for your choice.

Activity 8—A Specific Planet
You will need: Pencil, paper, books about planets.

Read a book or a chapter on a specific planet. Take notes
so that you can tell others what you learned about the
planet.

PURE SCIENCES:
ASTRONOMY

Adams, Richard. OUR AMAZING SUN. Illus. by Patti Boyd. Mahwah, New Jersey: Troll Assoc., 1983.

Adler, David. ALL ABOUT THE MOON. Illus. by Ray Burns. Mahwah, New Jersey: Troll Assoc., 1983.

Asimov, Isaac. ASTRONOMY TODAY. Milwaukee, Wisconsin: Gareth Stevens, Inc., 1989.

Asimov, Isaac. EARTH OUR HOME BASE. Milwaukee, Wisconsin: Gareth Stevens, Inc. 1988.

Bendick, Jeanne. ARTIFICIAL SATELLITES: HELPERS IN SPACE. New York: Millbrook Press, 1991.

Bendick, Jeanne. COMETS AND METEORS: VISITORS FROM SPACE. New York: Millbrook Press, 1991.

Brown, Robert and Brian Jones. EXPLORING SPACE. Milwaukee, Wisconsin: Gareth Stevens, Inc., 1989.

Darling, David J. COMETS, METEORS AND ASTEROIDS: ROCKS IN SPACE. New York: Macmillan Child Group, 1984.

Darling, David J. THE NEW ASTRONOMY: AN EVER-CHANGING UNIVERSE. New York: Macmillan Child Group, 1985.

Darling, David J. THE STARS FROM BIRTH TO BLACK HOLE. New York: Macmillan Child Group, 1985.

Darling, David J. WHERE ARE WE GOING IN SPACE? New York: Macmillan Child Group, 1984.

Hamer, Martyn. NIGHT SKY. New York: F. Watts, 1983.

Liptah, Karen. ASTRONOMY BASICS. New York: Prentice Hall, 1986.

Mammana, Dennis. THE NIGHT SKY: A GUIDE FOR THE YOUNG ASTRONOMER. Philadelphia: Running Press, 1989.

Marsh, Carole. ASTRONOMY FOR KIDS: MILKY WAY AND MARS BARS. Decatur, Georgia: Gallopade Pub. Group, 1990.

Simon, Seymour. GALAXIES. New York: Morrow Jr. Books, 1988.

Thompson, C. E. GLOW IN THE DARK CONSTELLATIONS: A FIELD GUIDE FOR YOUNG STARGAZERS. Illus. by Randy Chewning. New York: Putnam Pub. Group, 1989.

Wood, Robert W. THIRTY-NINE EASY ASTRONOMY EXPERIMENTS. Blue Ridge Summit, Pennsylvania: TAB Books, 1991.

600–699
TECHNOLOGY:
MEDICINE AND HEALTH

Activity 1—History of Medicine
You will need: Pencil, paper, a book about the history of medicine.

You have seen the physician's symbol, a stick with a snake twining around it. Read a book about the history of medicine to learn the meaning of this symbol. Draw and label a picture of the symbol and write at least three facts about its origin and meaning.

Activity 2—Time Line of Medical History
You will need: Pencil, paper, books about the history of medicine.

Read books about the history of medicine. Write at least five interesting things that you learned and make a time line showing important events or discoveries in the development of medicine.

Activity 3—A Famous Medical Person
You will need: Pencil, paper, books about famous people in medicine.

Read about a famous person in the medical field, such as a doctor, nurse, or researcher. Write a paragraph telling about the person and his/her contribution to the field of medicine.

Activity 4—Careers in the Medical Field
You will need: Pencil, paper, books about jobs in the medical profession.

Read a book about the many jobs existing in the medical world. List at least five of these jobs and write a sentence describing each of them.

Activity 5— Parts of the Body
You will need: Pencil, paper, books about the human body.

Select a part of the body such as the head or foot. Read a book about it. List three or more interesting things about the part of the body you selected.

600–699
TECHNOLOGY:
MEDICINE AND HEALTH

Activity 6—Interesting Medical Facts
You will need: Pencil, paper, books about medical facts.

Do you know what gives you goose bumps? Hiccups? Why does a body stop growing? Read books about some interesting medical facts. List at least five facts that you found interesting or that are new to you.

Activity 7—The Human Skeleton
You will need: Pencil, paper, a book about the human skeleton.

List and describe at least five of the following bones: ulna, tibia, clavicle, scapula, vertebra, patella, femur, radius, humerus, fibula.

Activity 8—The Digestive System
You will need: Pencil, paper, a book about the digestive system.

Read a book about what happens to food in your body during the process of digestion. Write a paragraph describing the process.

Activity 9—Sense of Taste
You will need: Pencil, paper, a book about the senses.

What is taste? Read a book or chapter about the sense of taste. Write a paragraph explaining this important sense.

Activity 10—Medical Instruments and Machines
You will need: Pencil, paper, books about instruments and machines of the medical field.

Read books about some of the instruments and machines that a doctor uses. List at least four of the following and tell what each is used for: thermometer, hypodermic syringe, stethoscope, x-ray, endoscope, forceps, laser. Draw pictures of the instruments/machines you choose to identify.

TECHNOLOGY:
MEDICINE AND HEALTH

Ardley, Bridget. SKIN, HAIR, TEETH. Englewood Cliffs, New Jersey: Silver Burdett Press, 1988.

Bailey, Donna. ALL ABOUT YOUR SENSES. Madison, New Jersey: Steck-V, 1990.

Behm, Barbara. THE STORY OF MEDICINE. Milwaukee, Wisconsin: Gareth Stevens, Inc., 1991.

Berger, Melvin. DISEASE DETECTIVES. New York: HarperCollins, 1978.

Berger, Melvin. GERMS MAKE ME SICK! Illus. by Marylin Hafner. New York: Thomas Crowell, 1985.

Bryan, Jenny. HEALTH AND SCIENCE. New York: Watts, 1988.

Bryan, Jenny. MEDICAL TECHNOLOGY. New York: Watts, 1991.

Carter, Adam. A DAY IN THE LIFE OF A MEDICAL DETECTIVE. Illus. by Bob Duncan. Mahwah, New Jersey: Troll Assoc., 1985.

Elting, Mary. THE MACMILLAN BOOK OF THE HUMAN BODY. Illus. by Kirk Moldoff. New York: Macmillan Books, 1986.

Giovanni, Caselli. THE HUMAN BODY. New York: Grosset, 1987.

Keable-Elliot, David. YOU AND YOUR BODY. Bedford, Virginia: Hamish, 1983.

Martin, M. W. LET'S TALK ABOUT THE NEW WORLD OF MEDICINE. Middle Village, New York: Jonathan David, 1973.

Parker, Steve. THE BRAIN AND NERVOUS SYSTEM. New York: Watts, 1990.

Parker, Steve. FOOD AND DIGESTION. New York: Watts, 1990.

Parker, Steve. THE HISTORY OF MEDICINE. Milwaukee, Wisconsin: Gareth Stevens, Inc., 1991.

Rowan, Peter. CAN YOU GET WARTS FROM TOUCHING TOADS? ASK DR. PETE. Englewood Cliffs, New Jersey: Messner, 1986.

Settel, Joanne and Nancy Baggett. WHY DOES MY NOSE RUN? AND OTHER QUESTIONS KIDS ASK ABOUT THEIR BODIES. Illus. by Linda Tunney. New York: Atheneum, 1985.

Showers, Paul. WHAT HAPPENS TO A HAMBURGER? Illus. by Anne Rockwell. New York HarperCollins, 1985.

Witty, Margot. A DAY IN THE LIFE OF AN EMERGENCY ROOM NURSE. Photos by Sarah Lewis. Mahwah, New Jersey: Troll Assoc., 1980.

600–699
TECHNOLOGY:
MEDICINE (CARE OF PETS)

Activity 1—How to Care for a Pet
You will need: Pencil, paper, books about caring for pets.

Read about how to care for a pet. Choose a pet, your own or one you would like to have, and write a plan for its proper care.

Activity 2—Imaginary Pet Story
You will need: Pencil, paper, a book about pets.

Read a book about a pet. Then write your own imaginary story about this pet.

Activity 3—Unusual Pets
You will need: Pencil, paper, books about pets.

Everyone knows about common pets such as dogs, cats, and horses. Many people, however, have more unusual pets. Read about the unusual animals that are kept as pets. Make a list of as many different kinds of pets as you can find. Draw a picture of one you would like to have as your pet.

Activity 4—Pet Similarities and Differences
You will need: Pencil, paper, books about pets.

Choose two pets. You may choose different animals such as a dog and a cat or you may choose two of the same general kind of animal, but different breeds such as a Labrador retriever and a poodle. Read about the animals' differences and similarities. Then make a chart showing these similarities and differences.

	SIMILARITIES	DIFFERENCES
PET A: _____		
PET B: _____		

600–699
TECHNOLOGY:
MEDICINE (CARE OF PETS)

Activity 5—Create a Pet Pamphlet
You will need: Pencil, paper, books on the care of pets.

Read as much as possible about the care of a specific pet. Create, write, and illustrate a pamphlet telling how to care for it. Draw a picture of the animal.

Activity 6—How to Train Your Pet
You will need: Pencil, paper, books on pets.

Read about the basic behavior training that almost any pet should have. Then choose a specific animal. Write a description of the proper way to train that animal. You may wish to go further and learn how to teach the animal to perform tricks or do particular tasks. Write another paragraph describing these procedures.

Activity 7—Animals Who Work
You will need: Pencil, paper, books about trained animals.

Some animals are trained to perform useful and often important tasks for people. Research as many examples as possible. Make a list of the animals and tell what each does to help people.

Activity 8—Rare and Unusual Pets
You will need: Pencil, paper, books about rare animals.

Read about several rare or unusual pets. Choose one. Pretend that you are a pet store owner or salesperson. Write a skit using the conversation between the salesperson and a customer who is interested in buying a pet. You will need to emphasize the animal's good points, such as personality and ease of care and feeding.

TECHNOLOGY:
MEDICINE (CARE OF PETS)

Bare, Colleen Stanley. TO LOVE A CAT. New York: Putnam, 1986

Bare, Colleen, Stanley. TO LOVE A DOG. New York: Putnam, 1987.

Berry, Joy W. TEACH ME ABOUT PETS. Danbury, Connecticut: Grolier, Inc., 1986.

Frisch, C. DUCKS. Vero Beach, Florida: Rourke Corp., 1991.

Frisch, C. PIGEONS. Vero Beach, Florida: Rourke Corp., 1991.

Hart, Angela. DOGS. New York: Franklin Watts, 1982.

Hearne, T. PARAKEETS. Vero Beach, Florida: Rourke Corp.,1991.

Herriot, James. BONNY'S BIG DAY. Illus. by Ruth Brown. New York: St. Martin's Press, 1987.

Hess, Lilo. MAKING FRIENDS WITH GUINEA PIGS: DIARY OF A RABBIT. New York: Scribners, 1983.

Hill, Rose. PETS AND PET CARE. Tulsa, Oklahoma: Educational Development Corp., 1983.

Hill, Rose. SMALL PETS. Tulsa, Oklahoma: Usborne, 1982.

Jameson, Pam and Tina Hearne. CATS: RESPONSIBLE PET CARE. Vero Beach, Florida: Rourke Corp., 1989.

Jameson, Pam and Tina Hearne. GERBILS: RESPONSIBLE PET CARE. Vero Beach, Florida: Rourke Corp., 1991.

McGrath, Susan. YOUR WORLD OF PETS. Illus. by Barbara L. Gibson. Washington, D.C.: The National Geographic Society, 1955.

Pope, Joyce. TAKING CARE OF YOUR GUNIEA PIG. New York: Franklin Watts, 1990.

Pope, Joyce. TAKING CARE OF YOUR HAMSTER. New York: Franklin Watts, 1986.

Posell, Elsa. HORSES. Chicago: Childrens Press, 1981.

Radlauer, Ed and Ruth Radlauer. PET MANIA. Chicago: Childrens Press, 1980.

Simon, Seymour. PETS IN A JAR: COLLECTING AND CARING FOR SMALL ANIMALS. Illus. by Betty Fraser. New York: Puffin Books, 1979.

Stevens, Carla. YOUR FIRST PET AND HOW TO TAKE CARE OF IT. New York: Macmillan, 1974.

Vrbova, ZuZa. JUNIOR PET CARE KOI FOR PONDS. Illus. by Robert McAulay. Neptune, New Jersey: TFH Pubns., 1990.

Watts, Barrie. HAMSTER. Morristown, New Jersey: Silver Burdett, 1986.

 700–799
THE ARTS:
PAINTING

Activity 1—Define Art Terms
You will need: Pencil, paper, a book about painting.

Read a book about painting. Use information in the text or glossary to define five or more of the following: fresco, still-life, palette, landscape, gold leaf, profile, pigment, easel, triptych, abstract painting, surrealist, modern.

Activity 2—Artists and Their Paintings
You will need: Pencil, paper, books about artists.

Read books about various artists. List the titles of at least six paintings, who painted them, and where the paintings are displayed.

Activity 3—Impressionist Painters
You will need: Pencil, paper, art materials, books with impressionistic paintings.

Study several pictures by impressionist painters such as Monet. Try drawing some familiar objects or people in this style. Think about how you are feeling and thinking as you create your impressionistic picture.

Activity 4—Leonardo da Vinci
You will need: Pencil, paper, a book about Leonardo da Vinci.

Find and study a picture of one of Leonardo da Vinci's paintings. Write a paragraph describing the painting.

Activity 5—American Painters

You will need: Pencil, paper, books about American painters.

Read books about American painters. Study some of the paintings. Most of them tell a story. Choose one of the paintings that you like and write a paragraph telling the painting's story.

Activity 6—Grandma Moses

You will need: Pencil, paper, crayons/markers or other art materials, a book about Grandma Moses.

Read a book or a chapter about the American painter known as Grandma Moses. How old was she when she started painting? Study some of her paintings. Create a scene in a similar style.

Activity 7—Different Styles of Painting

You will need: Pencil, paper, books about different paintings.

Study a number of paintings in different styles: portraits, still-lifes, landscapes, etc. Choose one painting that you especially like. Write its title and a paragraph describing the painting. Tell why you like it.

Activity 8—Famous Female Artist

You will need: Pencil, paper, a book about a female painter.

Read a book or article about a female painter. Then write an article for an imaginary newspaper about her and her artwork. Draw a picture to represent a newspaper photo of at least one of her paintings.

THE ARTS:
PAINTING

Badman, Jacqueline, Harriet Kinghorn and Lisa Lewis-Spicer. LET'S MEET FAMOUS ARTISTS. Minneapolis, Minnesota: T.S. Denison & Co., Inc., 1991.

Epstein, Vivian Sheldon. HISTORY OF WOMEN ARTISTS FOR CHILDREN. Denver, Colorado: VSE Pub., 1989.

Greenberg, Jan and Sandra Jordan. THE PAINTER'S EYE: LEARNING TO LOOK AT CONTEMPORARY AMERICAN ART. New York: Delacorte Press, 1991.

McLanathan, Richard. LEONARDO DA VINCI. New York: Harry N. Abrams, 1990.

Merymam, Richard. FIRST IMPRESSIONS: ANDREW WYETH. New York: Harry N. Abrams, 1991.

Meyer, Susan. FIRST IMPRESSIONS: MARY CASSATT. New York: Harry N. Abrams, 1990.

Peppin, Anthea. THE USBORNE STORY OF PAINTING. Illus. by Joseph McEwan. London: Usborne Pub., 1980.

Raboff, Ernest. MICHELANGELO. New York: J.B. Lippincott, 1988.

Richardson, Wendy and Jack Richardson. NATURAL WORLD: THROUGH THE EYES OF ARTISTS. Chicago: Childrens Press, 1991.

Richardson, Wendy and Jack Richardson. WATER: THROUGH THE EYES OF ARTISTS. Chicago: Childrens Press, 1991.

Roalf, Peggy. LOOKING AT PAINTINGS: CATS. New York: Hyperion Books for Children, 1992.

Roalf, Peggy. LOOKING AT PAINTINGS: SEASCAPES. New York: Hyperion Books for Children, 1992.

Rodari, Florian. A WEEKEND WITH PICASSO. New York: Rizzoli, 1991.

Skira-Venturi, Rosabianca. A WEEKEND WITH RENOIR. New York: Rizzoli, 1990.

Sullivan, Charles. IMAGINARY GARDENS: AMERICAN POETRY & ART FOR YOUNG PEOPLE. New York: Harry N. Abrams, 1989.

Turner, Robyn Montana. ROSA BONHEUR. Boston: Little, Brown, 1991.

Venezia, Mike. GETTING TO KNOW THE WORLD'S GREATEST ARTISTS: VAN GOGH. Chicago: Childrens Press, 1988.

Ventura, Piero. GREAT PAINTERS. New York: G.P. Putnam's, 1984.

Winter, Jeanette. DIEGO. New York: Knopf, 1991.

Woolf, Felicity. PICTURE THIS: A FIRST INTRODUCTION TO PAINTINGS. New York: Doubleday, 1989.

Yenawine, Philip. COLORS. New York: Delacorte Press, 1991.

 **700-799**
THE ARTS:
MUSIC

Activity 1—Orchestras
You will need: Pencil, paper, a book about orchestras.

Read a book about orchestras. What are the four main sections in an orchestra? Where do they sit? Draw and label a map to show where each section sits.

Activity 2—A Well-Known Musician
You will need: Pencil, paper, books about musicians.

Read a book about a well-known musician. Write five or more interesting facts that you learned about the person.

Activity 3—Rewrite a Favorite Tune
You will need: Pencil, paper, a songbook.

From a songbook, choose a tune that you know and like. Write new lyrics for that tune.

Activity 4—Conductors
You will need: Pencil, paper, books about orchestras.

Read about conductors. Write a paragraph about their job.

Activity 5—Musical Instruments
You will need: Pencil, paper, books on musical instruments.

Read a book about the four main groups of instruments. Make a chart showing at least three in each group.

700-799
THE ARTS: MUSIC

Activity 6—Dance
You will need: Pencil, paper, books about dance, a songbook.

Read books about dancing. The steps of a dance are usually shown as numbered footprints. Select a song from a songbook and make up a dance for it. Draw footprints with numbers on a piece of paper to show the order of the steps.

Activity 7—Different Kinds of Music
You will need: Pencil, paper, books about different kinds of music.

Read about different kinds of music. List at least three different kinds. What is your favorite kind of music? Write a paragraph telling why it is your favorite.

Activity 8—A Famous Composer
You will need: Pencil, paper, a book about a famous composer.

Read a book about a well-known composer. Write a paragraph about the composer, the kind of music he or she wrote and the title of one or more famous pieces by this composer.

Activity 9—Emotional Songs
You will need: Pencil, paper, songbooks.

Find and study songs that express a particular emotion such as joy, sadness, or love. Make a list of songs. After each title, name the emotion that you feel when you hear this song.

THE ARTS:
MUSIC

ABC: MUSICAL INSTRUMENTS FROM THE METROPOLITAN MUSEUM OF ART. New York: Harry N. Abrams, 1988.

Ardley, Neil. MUSIC. New York: Alfred A. Knopf, 1989.

Arnold, Caroline. MUSIC LESSONS FOR ALEX. Photos by Richard Hewett. Boston: Clarion Books, 1985.

Bryan, Ashley. WALK TOGETHER CHILDREN. New York: Antheneum, 1974.

Caney, Steven. TEACH YOURSELF TAP DANCING. New York: Workman Pub., 1991.

Carter, Eneida and Miriam Mikalac. BREAK DANCE: THE FREE AND EASY WAY! Illus. by Jan A. Forman. Philadelphia, Pennsylvania: Free and Easy Pub., 1984.

Downing, Julie. MOZART TONIGHT. New York: Bradbury, 1991.

Fichter, George S. AMERICAN INDIAN MUSIC AND MUSICAL INSTRUMENTS. New York: McKay, 1978.

Fleischman, Paul. RONDO IN C. Illus. by Janet Wentworth. New York: HarperCollins, 1988.

Greene, Carol. LUDWIG VAN BEETHOVEN: MUSICAL PIONEER. Chicago: Childrens Press, 1989.

Hayes, Ann. MEET THE ORCHESTRA. Illus. by Karmen Thompson. San Diego, California: Harcourt Brace Jovanovich, 1991.

Marks, Claude. GO IN AND OUT THE WINDOW. Cambridge, Massachusetts: Henry Holt, 1987.

McLean, Margaret. MAKE YOUR OWN MUSICAL INSTRUMENTS. Illus. by Ken Stott. Minneapolis, Minnesota: Learner Pub., 1988.

Michell, Barbara. AMERICA, I HEAR YOU: A STORY ABOUT GEORGE GERSHWIN. Illus. by Ian Hosking Smith. Minneapolis, Minnesota: Carolrhoda, 1987.

Storr, Catherine. THE NUTCRACKER: EASY PIANO PICTURE BOOK. (music by Tchaikovsky) Illus. by Dianne Jackson. London: Faber and Faber, 1987.

Taylor, Barbara. SOUND AND MUSIC. New York: Watts, 1991.

Ventura, Piero. GREAT COMPOSERS. New York: G.P. Putnam's Sons, 1989.

Weil, Lisl. THE MAGIC OF MUSIC. New York: Holiday House, 1989.

Weil, Lisl. WOLFERL: THE FIRST SIX YEARS IN THE LIFE OF WOLFGANG AMADEUS MOZART 1756-1762. New York: Holiday House, 1991.

800–899
LITERATURE:
POETRY

Activity 1—A Favorite Poem
You will need: Pencil, crayons/markers, paper, books of poetry.

Find and read at least two poems written by a poet of your choice. Write the name of the poet and the name of the poems on your paper. Choose the poem that you like best. Copy the poem neatly and draw pictures to illustrate it.

Activity 2—Anonymous Poet
You will need: Pencil, crayons/markers, paper, a book of poetry.

Look up the definition of an "anonymous" poet. Then find and read a poem by an anonymous poet. Copy it neatly on a sheet of paper. Draw a picture to illustrate the poem.

Activity 3—Poetry Anthology
You will need: Pencil, paper, a poetry anthology.

Look in the index of a poetry anthology and list three or more poets who have poems included in it. Read several poems by each of these authors. In your neatest handwriting, copy the poem that you like best. Then write a sentence or short paragraph telling why you chose this poem.

Activity 4—Rhyme Scheme
You will need: Pencil, paper, books of poetry.

Read several poems that have rhyming words at the ends of their lines. Notice the rhyme scheme (pattern). Which lines rhyme? Which ones do not? Now write a poem that rhymes.

The days of summer, lazy, long
On rippled pond with birds in song.
Are the days in which to sweetly dream
Of warmth, of joy, of forest stream.

800–899 LITERATURE: POETRY

Activity 5—Life of a Famous Poet

You will need: Pencil, paper, books on famous poets.

Read to learn about the life of a famous poet. Using the information you learned, write a biographical poem about this person.

Activity 6—Haiku

You will need: Pencil, paper, books containing poetry in the haiku form.

Haiku is a form of Japanese poetry. Nature and seasons are usually the subject of haiku poetry. A haiku poem always contains three lines with five syllables in the first line, seven in the second line, and five in the third line.

> Birds sing, flowers bloom.
> The sun gently warms the earth.
> Spring has come again.

Find and read some examples of this form of poetry. Then write at least one of your own poems in the haiku form.

Activity 7—Stanzas

You will need: Pencil, paper, books of poetry.

Look up the word *stanza*. Write its definition on a sheet of paper. Find a poem that you like. Notice the rhyme pattern and the meter (the pattern of stressed and unstressed syllables). Write another stanza for the poem.

Activity 8—Illustrate a Poem

You will need: Pencil, paper, poetry books.

Read three or more poems. Neatly copy and illustrate one or more of them.

LITERATURE:
POETRY

Brown, Ruth. LADYBUG, LADYBUG. New York: E. P. Dutton, 1988.

Chapman, Jean, comp. CAT WILL RHYME WITH HAT: A BOOK OF POEMS. Illus. by Peter Parnall. New York: Charles Scribner's Sons, 1986.

Coleridge, Sara. JANUARY BRINGS THE SNOW: A BOOK OF MONTHS. Illus. by Jenni Oliver. New York: Dial Books for Young Readers, 1986.

de Regniers, Beatrice Schenk, et al., comp. SING A SONG OF POPCORN: EVERY CHILD'S BOOK OF POEMS. Illus. by Marcia Brown. New York: Scholastic, 1988.

de Regniers, Beatrice Schenk. THE WAY I FEEL...SOMETIMES. Illus. by Susan Meddaugh. New York: Clarion Books, 1988.

Dragonwagon, Crescent. HALF A MOON AND ONE WHOLE STAR. Illus. by Jerry Pinkney. New York: Macmillan, 1986.

Fisher, Aileen. WHEN IT COMES TO BUGS. Illus. by Chris Degen and Bruce Degen. New York: Harper and Row, 1986.

Fleischman, Paul. I AM PHOENIX: POEMS FOR TWO VOICES. Illus. by Ken Nutt. New York: HarperCollins, 1985.

Greenfield, Eloise. UNDER THE SUNDAY TREE. Illus. by Amos Ferguson. New York: Harper and Row, 1988.

Hooper, Patricia. A BUNDLE OF BEASTS. Illus. by Mark Steele. New York: Houghton Mifflin, 1987.

Hopkins, Lee Bennett, comp. CLICK, RUMBLE, ROAR: POEMS ABOUT MACHINES. Photographs by Anna Held Audette. New York: Thomas Y. Crowell, 1987.

Hubbell, Patricia. THE TIGER BROUGHT PINK LEMONADE. Illus. by Ju-Hong Chen. New York: Atheneum, 1988.

Janeczko, Paul B., comp. THIS DELICIOUS DAY. New York: Orchard Books, 1987.

Larrick, Nancy, comp. CATS ARE CATS. Illus. by Ed Young. New York: Philomel Books, 1988.

Lear, Edward. THE OWL AND THE PUSSYCAT. Illus. by Paul Galdone. New York: Clarion Books, 1987.

Little, Lessie Jones. CHILDREN OF LONG AGO: POEMS. Illus. by Jan Spivey Gilchrist. New York: Philomel Books, 1988.

Livingston, Myra Cohn. CELEBRATIONS. Illus. by Leonard Everett Fisher. New York: Holiday House, 1985.

Merriam, Eve. BLACKBERRY INK. Illus. by Hans Wilhelm. New York: William Morrow, 1985.

 **800–899**
LITERATURE:
PLAYS

Activity 1—Character Descriptions
You will need: Pencil, paper, play book.

Read a play. Write a description of each of the characters in the play. Reread the play to see if the characters seem more familiar to you after a second reading. List the title of the play book you read.

Activity 2—From a Play to a Short Story
You will need: Pencil, paper, play books.

Read at least two plays. Then rewrite one of the plays as a story. You may write the story using your own creative thoughts or you may write your story using the story line from the play.

Activity 3—The Main Character
You will need: Pencil, paper, a play book.

Read a play. Study the main character of the play. What, for example, does he/she/it look like? Approximately how old is the main character? What does the main character like to do? Write a short biography of the main character in the play.

Activity 4—"Play Starter"
You will need: Pencil, paper, play book that includes a table of contents.

Look at the table of contents of play titles in a play book. Use a title of a play that you haven't read as a "Play Starter." Write a play based on the title. After you have written your play, read the original play from the book. How is your play similar to the original play? How is it different?

800–899
LITERATURE:
PLAYS

Activity 5—Format of Skits
You will need: Pencil, paper, books on skits.

Read and study the format of skits. Then create and write your own skit. Use any characters that you want.

Activity 6—Write a New Ending
You will need: Pencil, paper, play books.

Read one or more plays. Then write a different ending to one of the plays. Will it be a funny ending, a sad ending, or a happy ending?

Activity 7—Puppet Plays
You will need: Pencil, paper, and puppet play book.

Read puppet plays. Create and write a puppet play of your own. Then create some puppets for your play. (Stick puppets, paper bag puppets, etc.) Share your play with the class.

Activity 8—Bibliography of Plays
You will need: Pencil, paper, play books.

Write a bibliography of the play books in your library. Draw a star by the ones that you read. Include the name of the author, the title, where the publisher is located, the name of the publisher, and the publication date. Can you locate on a map the place where each book was published?

Example for bibliography:

Adorjan, Carol and Yuri Rasovsky. WKID: EASY RA-DIO PLAYS. Niles, Illinois: Albert Whitman and Company, 1988.

LITERATURE:
PLAYS

Adorjan, Carol and Yuri Rasovshy. WKID: EASY RADIO PLAYS. Niles, Illinois: Albert Whitman and Company, 1988.

Alexander, Sue. SMALL PLAYS FOR SPECIAL DAYS. llus. by Tom Huffman. New York: Houghton Mifflin, 1979.

Ayckbourn, Alan. MR. A'S AMAZING MAZE PLAYS. Winchester, Maryland: Faber and Faber, 1990.

Bellville, Cheryl W. THEATER MAGIC: BEHIND THE SCENES AT A CHILDREN'S THEATER. New York: Carolrhoda, 1986.

Birch, Beverly. SHAKESPEARE'S STORIES: COMEDIES. Illus. by Carol Tarrant. New York: P. Bedrick Books, 1988.

Boiko, Claire. CHILDREN'S PLAYS FOR CREATIVE ACTORS. Boston: Plays, 1985.

Brooks, Courtaney. THE CASE OF THE STOLEN DINOSAUR: A PLAY IN TWO VERSIONS: STAGE AND RADIO. Illus. by Merrilee Way. Manhattan Beach, California: Belnice Books, 1983.

Brooks, Courtaney. LITTLE RED AND THE WOLF: A PUPPET PLAY. Illus. by Merrilee Way. Manhattan Beach, California. Belnice Books, 1983.

Brooks, Courtaney. PARDNER AND FREDDIE: A PUPPET PLAY. Illus. by Merrilee Way. Manhattan Beach, California. Belnice Books, 1983.

Bush, Max. THE VOYAGE OF THE DRAGONFLY. New Orleans, Louisana: Anchorage, 1989.

Chorpenning, Charlotte B.. THE ADVENTURES OF TOM SAWYER. Woodstock, Illinois: Dramatic Pub., 1956.

Dahl, Roald. CHARLIE AND THE CHOCOLATE FACTORY. Illus. by Joseph Schindelman. New York: Knopf, 1991.

Dunster, Mark. CHIMNEY. Hollywood, California: Linden Pub., 1990.

Fisher, Aileen. YEAR-ROUND PROGRAMS FOR YOUNG PLAYERS. Boston: Plays, 1985.

Havilan, Amorie and Lyn Smith. EASY PLAYS FOR PRESCHOOLERS TO THIRD GRADERS. Brandon, Mississippi: Quail Ridge, 1986.

Haycock, Kate. PLAYS. Ada, Oklahoma: Garrett Ed Corp., 1991.

Kline, Suzy. THE HERBIE JONES READER'S THEATER. Illus. by Richard Williams. New York: G.P. Putnam's Sons, 1992.

Rockwell, Thomas. HOW TO EAT FRIED WORMS AND OTHER PLAYS. Illus. by Joel Schick. New York: Delacorte, 1980.

900–999
GENERAL GEOGRAPHY AND HISTORY:
BIOGRAPHY/AUTOBIOGRAPHY

Activity 1—Make a List of Biographies/Autobiographies
You will need: Pencil, paper, biographies or autobiographies.

In your classroom, school, or other library, find a biography (or autobiography) of someone from each of the following groups: artists, writers, entertainers, explorers, scientists, inventors, and politicians. List the titles of the books that you find. Read one or more of these books. Draw a star beside each one that you read.

Activity 2—A Famous Person
You will need: Pencil, paper, a biography.

Read about a famous person whom you find interesting. Draw a portrait of this person.

Activity 3—My Own Biography
You will need: Pencil, paper, biographies.

Read one or more biographies. Biographies are written because people enjoy reading about others who have led interesting lives. They may have accomplished important things, had some great adventure, or overcome a handicap that causes admiration. Think about your life. Write a paragraph telling what you would like a biographer to write about you.

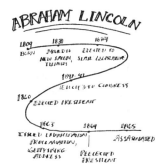

Activity 4—Biographical Time Line
You will need: Pencil, paper, an autobiography or biography.

Read an autobiography or a biography. Make a time line diagramming the lifetime events of the person you read about.

Example: Illustration of a time line of someone that everyone would know something about—such as Abe Lincoln.

Activity 5—Writing Biographical Facts
You will need: Pencil, paper, a biography.

Read a biography or an autobiography. Write six or more interesting facts that you learned about this person's life.

Activity 6—Write Your Own Autobiography
You will need: Pencil, paper, an autobiography.

An autobiography is the story of a person's own life written by himself/herself. Read an autobiography. Write your own autobiography. Include interesting things that have happened to you or that you have done.

Activity 7—Biography Poetry
You will need: Pencil, paper, a biography.

Read a biography. Write the person's full name down the side of a piece of paper. Using the letters of the person's name as the first letters of the lines, write facts you have learned about him or her.

Example: (This is a sample started for "Ben Franklin.")
Born in Boston in 1706
Editor, statesman, scientist
New glasses, and bifocals are only two of his inventions.

Activity 8—Biography Alphabet List
You will need: Pencil, paper, biographies.

List the letters of the alphabet down the left side of a piece of paper. In your classroom, school, or other library, look for biographies of people whose last names begin with these letters. Fill as many lines as you can. Give yourself one point for each line you fill.
A. Anthony, Susan B.
B.

GENERAL GEOGRAPHY AND HISTORY:
BIOGRAPHY

Anderson, LaVere. MARTHA WASHINGTON: FIRST LADY OF THE LAND. Illus. by Cary. New York: Chelsea House, 1991.

Behrens, June. JULIETTE LOW: FOUNDER OF THE GIRL SCOUTS OF AMERICA. Chicago: Childrens Press, 1988.

Clarke, Brenda. CARING FOR OTHERS. Austin, Texas: Steck-V., 1990.

Dunn, Andrew. ALEXANDER GRAHAM BELL: INVENTOR OF THE TELEPHONE. New York: Watts, 1991.

FAMOUS MEN AND WOMEN. Milwaukee, Wisconsin: Raintree Pub., 1987.

Ferris, Jeri. NATIVE AMERICAN DOCTOR: THE STORY OF SUSAN LA FLESCHE PICOTTE. Minneapolis, Minnesota: Carolrhoda, 1991.

Fritz, Jean. AND THEN WHAT HAPPENED, PAUL REVERE? Illus. by Margot Tomes. New York: Coward, 1982.

Freedman, Russell. LINCOLN: A PHOTOBIOGRAPHY. New York: Clarion Books, 1987.

Goodwin, Bob and Dympna Hayes. FAMOUS LIVES. Niagra Falls, NY: Durkin Hayes Pub., 1987.

Latham, Jean L. ELIZABETH BLACKWELL: PIONEER WOMAN DOCTOR. Illus. by Ethel Gold. New York: Chelsea House. 1991.

Levinson, Nancy S. CHUCK YEAGER: THE MAN WHO BROKE THE SOUND BARRIER. New York: Walker, 1988.

McLeish, Kenneth and Valerie McLeish. FAMOUS PEOPLE. Mahwah, New Jersey: Troll Assocs., 1990.

Meryman, Richard. ANDREW WYETH: FIRST IMPRESSIONS SERIES. New York: Harry N. Abrams, 1991.

Mitchell, Barbara. SHOES FOR EVERYONE: A STORY ABOUT JAN MATZELIGER. Minneapolis, Minnesota: Carolrhoda Books, Inc., 1986.

Osborne, Mary P. GEORGE WASHINGTON: LEADER OF A NEW NATION. New York: Dial Books, 1991.

Peavy, Linda and Ursula Smith. WOMEN WHO CHANGED THINGS. New York: Scribner, 1983.

PEOPLE WHO HAVE HELPED THE WORLD (24 vols.). Milwaukee, Wisconsin: Gareth Stevens Inc., 1987.

Schroeder, Alan. BOOKER T. WASHINGTON. New York: Chelsea House, 1992.

Tanenhaus, Sam. LOUIS ARMSTRONG, MUSICIAN. New York: Chelsea House Pub., 1989.

900–999
GENERAL GEOGRAPHY AND HISTORY: GEOGRAPHY

Activity 1—An Asian Country
You will need: Pencil, paper, a book about an Asian country.

Asia is the largest continent and consists of many countries including China, India, Japan, and Saudi Arabia. Read a book about an Asian country. List five or more interesting facts that you learned from your reading.

Activity 2—A European Country
You will need: Pencil, crayons, paper, books about a European country.

Read books about a European country and draw at least three pictures showing native costumes, arts/crafts, musical instruments, or other interesting features of the country you chose. Label the pictures.

Activity 3—Australian Words
You will need: Pencil, paper, books about Australia.

Australia is the world's smallest continent. Although Australians speak English, some of their words and expressions are only heard in Australia. Read about this country. Then list five of these unique words or expressions and their meanings. Include the sources and page numbers to show where you found this information.

Activity 4—Animals of Africa
You will need: Pencil, crayons/markers, paper, books about Africa.

Africa is known for its wild animals. Read about the animals of Africa. Then draw pictures of at least three animals that you find most interesting. Under each picture, write several facts that you discovered about each animal.

Activity 5—Life in Antarctica
You will need: Pencil, crayons/markers, paper, books about Antarctica.

The continent of Antarctica has the coldest temperatures of any place on earth. Read about this continent. Then make a chart of the plants and animals of Antarctica.

Activity 6—Mexican Marketplace
You will need: Pencil, crayons/markers, paper, books about Mexico.

Many cities in Mexico have markets where farmers, crafts-people, and merchants gather to sell their products. Read books about Mexico to learn about the kinds of farm produce and other products of this country. Then draw a marketplace showing how these products are sold.

Activity 7—A South American Country
You will need: Pencil, paper, a book about South America.

Read a book about South America or a South American country. Make a list of its agricultural (farm) products. Organize your list from most important to least important products. Write the title of your source (and page number) to show where you found this information.

Activity 8—Canadian Poetry
You will need: Pencil, paper, a book about Canada.

Read a book about Canada. Make an acrostic poem by printing the word "Canada" down one side of a piece of paper. Use each of the letters as the first letters in a sentence or phrase. Use facts you've learned about this North American country.

GENERAL GEOGRAPHY AND HISTORY:
GEOGRAPHY

ANTARCTICA. New York: S & S Trade, 1991.

Bains, Rae. EUROPE. Illus. by Allan Eitzen. Mahwah, New Jersey: Troll Assoc., 1985.

Baynham, Simon. AFRICA. New York: F. Watts, 1987.

Bender, Lionel. CANADA. Englewood Cliffs, New Jersey: Silver Burdett, 1988.

Chiasson, John. AFRICAN JOURNEY. New York: Macmillan Children's Group, 1987.

Cranshaw, Peter. AUSTRALIA. Englewood Cliffs, New Jersey: Silver Burdett, 1988.

Dempsey, Michael. STUDENT ATLAS. Mahwah, New Jersey: Troll Assoc., 1991.

Fairfield, Sheila. PEOPLE AND NATIONS OF ASIA. Milwaukee, Wisconsin: Gareth Stevens, Inc., 1988.

Fairfield, Sheila. PEOPLE AND NATIONS OF EUROPE. Milwaukee, Wisconsin: Gareth Stevens, Inc., 1988.

Garrett, Dan and Grinrod, Warril. AUSTRALIA. Austin, Texas: Steck-V, 1990.

Georges, D. V. ASIA. Chicago: Childrens Press, 1986.

GETTING TO KNOW MEXICO. Lincolnwood, Illinois: National Textbook, 1990.

Henry-Biabaud, Chantal. LIVING IN SOUTH AMERICA. Ossining, New York: Young Discovery Lib., 1991.

James, Ian. MEXICO. New York: F. Watts, 1989.

Knowlton, Jack. GEOGRAPHY FROM A TO Z. Illus. by Harriett Barton. New York: Crowell Jr., 1988.

PICTURE ATLAS OF THE WORLD. Illus. by Brian Delf. Chicago: Rand McNally, 1991.

Roberts, Elizabeth. EUROPE. New York: F. Watts, 1992.

Stanley-Baker, Penny. AUSTRALIA: ON THE OTHER SIDE OF THE WORLD. Illus. by Pierre-Marie Valat. Ossining, New York: Young Discovery Lib., 1988.

Swan, Robert. DESTINATION: ANTARCTICA. Photos by John Chiasson. New York: Scholastic, 1988.

THE USBORNE BOOK OF WORLD GEOGRAPHY. Tulsa, Oklahoma: Usborne Pub., 1987.

INDEPENDENT ACTIVITIES

Read books on a specific topic. Then create and write your own independent activities for others to do. Write the answers on a separate sheet of paper. Use the back of this sheet of paper if you need more space for the activities.

Your Name: _____ Date: _____

Topic: _____ Dewey Decimal Section: _____

Materials Needed: _____

ACTIVITIES

1. _____

_____

_____

_____

_____

_____

_____

SOURCE USED: _____

****

2. _____

_____

_____

_____

_____

_____

_____

SOURCE USED: _____

000–099

DEWEY DECIMAL CHART

000 Generalities

010   **Bibliographies & Catalogs**

020   **Library & Information Sciences**

030   **General Encyclopedia Works**

050   **General Serial Publications**

060   **General Organizations & Museology**

070   **Journalism, Publishing, Newspapers**

080   **General Collections**

090   **Manuscripts & Book Rarities**

**000–099 GENERALITIES
(ENCYCLOPEDIAS, BIBLIOGRAPHIES, PERIODICALS, JOURNALISM)**

100–199
DEWEY DECIMAL CHART

100 Philosophy & Related Disciplines

110   Metaphysics

120   Knowledge, Cause, Purpose, Man

130   Popular & Parapsychology

140   Specific Philosophical Viewpoints

150   Psychology

160   Logic

170   Ethics (Moral Philosophy)

180   Ancient, Medieval, Oriental

190   Modern Western Philosophy

**100–199 PHILOSOPHY AND RELATED DISCIPLINES
(PHILOSOPHY, PSYCHOLOGY, LOGIC)**

Color, cut, and display this chart.

200–299
DEWEY DECIMAL CHART

200 Religion

210	Natural Religion
220	Bible
230	Christian Doctrinal Theology
240	Christian Moral & Devotional
250	Local Church & Religious Orders
260	Social & Ecclesiastical Theology
270	History & Geography of Church
280	Christian Denominations & Sects
290	Other Religions & Comparative

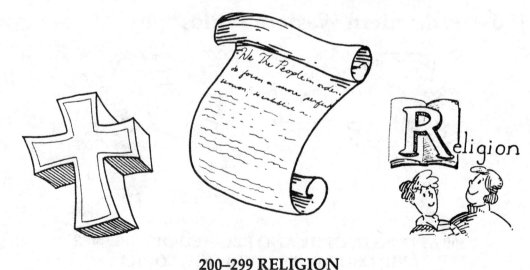

200–299 RELIGION

300–399

DEWEY DECIMAL CHART

300 The Social Sciences

310   Statistics

320   Political Science

330   Economics

340   Law

350   Public Administration

360   Social Pathology & Services

370   Education

380   Commerce

390   Customs & Folklore

**300–399 THE SOCIAL SCIENCES
(ECONOMICS, SOCIOLOGY, CIVICS, LAW,
EDUCATION, VOCATIONS, CUSTOMS)**

400–499
DEWEY DECIMAL CHART

Si̇l-ə-bəls

400 Language

410   Linguistics

420   English & Anglo-Saxon Languages

430   Germanic Languages — German

440   Romance Languages — French

450   Italian, Romanian, Rhaeto-Romanic

460   Spanish & Portuguese Languages

470   Italic Languages — Latin

480   Hellenic — Classical Greek

490   Other Languages

400–499 LANGUAGE
(LANGUAGE, DICTIONARIES, GRAMMAR)

500–599

DEWEY DECIMAL CHART

500 Pure Sciences

510	Mathematics
520	Astronomy & Allied Sciences
530	Physics
540	Chemistry & Allied Sciences
550	Sciences of Earth & Other Worlds
560	Paleontology
570	Life Sciences
580	Botanical Sciences
590	Zoological Sciences

500–599 PURE SCIENCES
(MATHEMATICS, ASTRONOMY, PHYSICS, CHEMISTRY,
GEOLOGY, PALEONTOLOGY, BIOLOGY, ZOOLOGY, BOTANY)

600–699
DEWEY DECIMAL CHART

600 Technology (Applied Sciences)

610   **Medical Sciences**

620   **Engineering & Allied Operations**

630   **Agriculture & Related**

640   **Domestic Arts & Sciences**

650   **Managerial Services**

660   **Chemical & Related Technologies**

670   **Manufactures**

680   **Miscellaneous Manufactures**

690   **Buildings**

600–699 TECHNOLOGY
(MEDICINE, ENGINEERING, AGRICULTURE, HOME ECONOMICS,
BUSINESS, RADIO, TELEVISION, AVIATION)

700–799

DEWEY DECIMAL CHART

700 The Arts

710	Civic & Landscape Art
720	Architecture
730	Plastic Arts — Sculpture
740	Drawing, Decorative & Minor Arts
750	Painting & Paintings
760	Graphic Arts — Prints
770	Photography & Photographs
780	Music
790	Recreational & Performing Arts

**700–799 THE ARTS
(ARCHITECTURE, SCULPTURE, PAINTING,
MUSIC, PHOTOGRAPHY, RECREATION)**

800–899
DEWEY DECIMAL CHART

800 Literature

810	**American Literature in English**
820	**English & Anglo-Saxon Literatures**
830	**Literature of Germanic Languages**
840	**Literature of Romance Languages**
850	**Italian, Romanian, Rhaeto-Romanic**
860	**Spanish & Portuguese Literatures**
870	**Italic Languages Literatures — Latin**
880	**Hellenic Languages Literatures**
890	**Literatures of Other Languages**

**800–899 LITERATURE
(NOVELS, POETRY, PLAYS, CRITICISM)**

900–999

DEWEY DECIMAL CHART

900 General Geography & History

910   General Geography — Travel

920   General Biography & Genealogy

930   General History of Ancient World

940   General History of Europe

950   General History of Asia

960   General History of Africa

970   General History of North America

980   General History of South America

990   General History of Other Areas

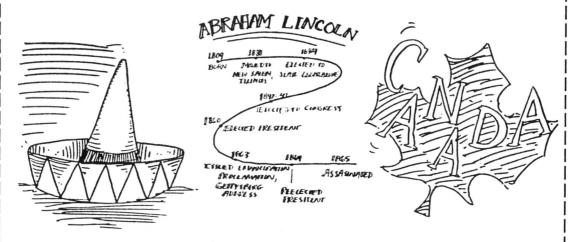

900–999 GENERAL GEOGRAPHY AND HISTORY